I am...

the author

Ke'sha Dennis is a serial entrepreneur with a passion for financial literacy and wealth building. From her early experiences in Oakland, California, Ke'sha developed a keen understanding of the economic challenges facing families. Influenced by care of her grandmother, she began her college education in search of a nursing degree. She discovered a more specific calling in leadership and entrepreneurship. After some success in the corporate world, Ke'sha became a tax professional and found her way into the financial arena with the realization of the immense impact finances play on health and well-being. With that foundation, she has continued to develop her ventures into multiple areas of women's empowerment including entrepreneurship, life coaching, financial coaching and spirituality. Ke'sha believes that self-development is the key to health, well-being and financial understanding. People can change their relationship with money, if they understand how money works and put in the work to make their money work for them. Ke'sha is living proof of the ability to transform your mindset in relation to finances.

Ke'sha founded Upscale Tax Professionals, creating a financial educational platform for fellow entrepreneurs to expand and grow exponentially. Upscale Tax Professionals has grown into a family of business owners on a mission to help others succeed within their own company's. Providing business entity filing, tax education, tax planning, tax preparation, notary public, nonprofit filing, financial consulting, bookkeeping, tax amendments and much more. Upscale Tax Professionals gains momentum in the world of finances daily by helping other business owners become financially operational wealth building establishments. Ke'sha's recently formulated, Lady Buzz Conversations That Create Movement. Lady Buzz is a non-profit that has a Facebook community with over 5000 members. She sponsors the group to promote conversations that create movement, having noticed that entrepreneurs needed a space to exchange their expertise and network with other influencers. The site is active with dozens of posts per day. Businesses are networking, profiting and growing in high numbers, driving a larger audience to their business page causing each business to flourish.

- ke'sha dennis
- kesha_dennis
- keshadennis7
- Upscale Tax Professionals Ke'sha Dennis

www.upscaletaxprofessionals.com

I am... What I am...

As the world continues to change and is very unpredictable, I choose to grow, to love, to live. As the earth evolves, so do I.

I know who I am and who I am not, and I celebrate the wholeness and abundance in my being.

I am grateful for everything that I have and everything I have yet to learn.

I know that life requires me to continually grow towards becoming more than the person I am today - my best version.

No matter what life throws at me, I place myself in full surrender.

I am and I can be more.

Monthly Planner

MONTH:

MON	TUE	WED	THU	FRI	SAT	SUN

GOALS:

NOTES:

DATE   /   /

today

to-do

notes   DATE   /   /

DATE / /

today　　　　　　　　　*to-do*

notes

DATE / /

DATE   /   /

today

to-do

- [ ]
- [ ]
- [ ]
- [ ]
- [ ]
- [ ]
- [ ]
- [ ]
- [ ]
- [ ]
- [ ]
- [ ]
- [ ]
- [ ]
- [ ]
- [ ]
- [ ]
- [ ]
- [ ]
- [ ]

notes DATE / /

DATE   /   /

today

to-do

notes

DATE   /   /

DATE   /   /

today   *to-do*

notes

DATE   /   /

DATE   /   /

today   *to-do*

notes

DATE / /

DATE   /   /

today

to-do

notes

DATE   /   /

Monthly Planner

MONTH:

MON	TUE	WED	THU	FRI	SAT	SUN

GOALS:

NOTES:

_____

_____

_____

_____

DATE   /   /

today

to-do

- [ ]
- [ ]
- [ ]
- [ ]
- [ ]
- [ ]
- [ ]
- [ ]
- [ ]
- [ ]
- [ ]
- [ ]
- [ ]
- [ ]
- [ ]
- [ ]
- [ ]
- [ ]
- [ ]
- [ ]

notes

DATE / /

DATE   /   /

today

to-do

- [ ]
- [ ]
- [ ]
- [ ]
- [ ]
- [ ]
- [ ]
- [ ]
- [ ]
- [ ]
- [ ]
- [ ]
- [ ]
- [ ]
- [ ]
- [ ]
- [ ]
- [ ]
- [ ]

notes

DATE / /

DATE   /   /

today

to-do

- [ ]
- [ ]
- [ ]
- [ ]
- [ ]
- [ ]
- [ ]
- [ ]
- [ ]
- [ ]
- [ ]
- [ ]
- [ ]
- [ ]
- [ ]
- [ ]
- [ ]
- [ ]
- [ ]
- [ ]

notes

DATE / /

DATE   /   /

today

to-do

notes

DATE / /

DATE   /   /

today

to-do

- [ ]
- [ ]
- [ ]
- [ ]
- [ ]
- [ ]
- [ ]
- [ ]
- [ ]
- [ ]
- [ ]
- [ ]
- [ ]
- [ ]
- [ ]
- [ ]
- [ ]
- [ ]
- [ ]

notes

DATE   /   /

DATE   /   /

today

to-do

- [ ]
- [ ]
- [ ]
- [ ]
- [ ]
- [ ]
- [ ]
- [ ]
- [ ]
- [ ]
- [ ]
- [ ]
- [ ]
- [ ]
- [ ]
- [ ]
- [ ]
- [ ]
- [ ]

notes

DATE   /   /

DATE   /   /

today

to-do

- [ ]
- [ ]
- [ ]
- [ ]
- [ ]
- [ ]
- [ ]
- [ ]
- [ ]
- [ ]
- [ ]
- [ ]
- [ ]
- [ ]
- [ ]
- [ ]
- [ ]
- [ ]
- [ ]
- [ ]

notes

DATE / /

Monthly Planner

MONTH:

MON	TUE	WED	THU	FRI	SAT	SUN

GOALS:

NOTES:

DATE ___ / ___ / ___

today

to-do

notes

DATE / /

DATE / /

today *to-do*

notes

DATE / /

DATE   /   /

today

to-do

notes

DATE   /   /

DATE   /   /

today

to-do

notes

DATE / /

DATE   /   /

today

to-do

notes

DATE   /   /

DATE   /   /

today

to-do

notes

DATE   /   /

DATE   /   /

today

to-do

notes

DATE   /   /

Monthly Planner

MONTH:

MON	TUE	WED	THU	FRI	SAT	SUN

GOALS:

NOTES:

_____

_____

_____

_____

DATE   /   /

today

to-do

notes　　　　　　　　　　　　DATE　　/　　/

DATE / /

today

to-do

notes

DATE   /   /

DATE   /   /

today

to-do

notes

DATE   /   /

DATE   /   /

today

to-do

- [ ]
- [ ]
- [ ]
- [ ]
- [ ]
- [ ]
- [ ]
- [ ]
- [ ]
- [ ]
- [ ]
- [ ]
- [ ]
- [ ]
- [ ]
- [ ]
- [ ]
- [ ]
- [ ]
- [ ]

notes

DATE   /   /

notes

DATE   /   /

DATE   /   /

today

to-do

- [ ]
- [ ]
- [ ]
- [ ]
- [ ]
- [ ]
- [ ]
- [ ]
- [ ]
- [ ]
- [ ]
- [ ]
- [ ]
- [ ]
- [ ]
- [ ]
- [ ]
- [ ]
- [ ]
- [ ]

notes

DATE / /

DATE   /   /

today

to-do

notes

DATE   /   /

DATE   /   /

today

to-do

- [ ]
- [ ]
- [ ]
- [ ]
- [ ]
- [ ]
- [ ]
- [ ]
- [ ]
- [ ]
- [ ]
- [ ]
- [ ]
- [ ]
- [ ]
- [ ]
- [ ]
- [ ]
- [ ]
- [ ]

notes

DATE / /

Monthly Planner

MONTH:

MON	TUE	WED	THU	FRI	SAT	SUN

GOALS:

NOTES:

_____

_____

_____

_____

DATE   /   /

today

to-do

- [ ]
- [ ]
- [ ]
- [ ]
- [ ]
- [ ]
- [ ]
- [ ]
- [ ]
- [ ]
- [ ]
- [ ]
- [ ]
- [ ]
- [ ]
- [ ]
- [ ]
- [ ]
- [ ]

notes   DATE   /   /

DATE   /   /

today

to-do

- [ ]
- [ ]
- [ ]
- [ ]
- [ ]
- [ ]
- [ ]
- [ ]
- [ ]
- [ ]
- [ ]
- [ ]
- [ ]
- [ ]
- [ ]
- [ ]
- [ ]
- [ ]
- [ ]

notes

DATE   /   /

DATE   /   /

today

to-do

- [ ]
- [ ]
- [ ]
- [ ]
- [ ]
- [ ]
- [ ]
- [ ]
- [ ]
- [ ]
- [ ]
- [ ]
- [ ]
- [ ]
- [ ]
- [ ]
- [ ]
- [ ]
- [ ]
- [ ]
- [ ]

notes

DATE   /   /

DATE   /   /

today

to-do

notes

DATE / /

DATE   /   /

today

to-do

notes

DATE / /

DATE   /   /

today

to-do

notes

DATE   /   /

DATE   /   /

today

to-do

notes   DATE   /   /

notes

DATE / /

notes

DATE   /   /

notes

DATE   /   /

notes

DATE   /   /

notes

DATE   /   /

notes

DATE   /   /

notes

DATE   /   /

notes

DATE   /   /

notes

DATE / /

notes

DATE   /   /

notes

DATE   /   /

notes

DATE / /

notes

DATE   /   /

notes

DATE   /   /

notes

DATE   /   /

notes

DATE / /

notes

DATE / /

notes

DATE   /   /

notes

DATE   /   /

notes

DATE   /   /

notes

DATE   /   /

www.ingramcontent.com/pod-product-compliance
Lightning Source LLC
Chambersburg PA
CBHW080552170426
43195CB00016B/2767